© Copyright 2001 Jim Drummond. All rights reserved.

No part of this publication may be reproduced, stored in a retrieval system, or transmitted, in any form or by any means, electronic, mechanical, photocopying, recording, or otherwise, without the written prior permission of the author.

National Library of Canada Cataloguing in Publication Data

Drummond, Jim.
  Selling power
  Includes bibliographical references.
  ISBN 1-55212-853-9

  1. Energy industries--Marketing. I. Hanna, Fred. II. Title.
HD9502.A2D78 2001   621.042'068'8   C2001-911052-9

TRAFFORD

This book was published *on-demand* in cooperation with Trafford Publishing.
On-demand publishing is a unique process and service of making a book available for retail sale to the public taking advantage of on-demand manufacturing and Internet marketing.
On-demand publishing includes promotions, retail sales, manufacturing, order fulfilment, accounting and collecting royalties on behalf of the author.

Suite 6E, 2333 Government St., Victoria, B.C. V8T 4P4, CANADA
Phone   250-383-6864   Toll-free 1-888-232-4444 (Canada & US)
Fax   250-383-6804   E-mail   sales@trafford.com
Web site www.trafford.com   TRAFFORD PUBLISHING IS A DIVISION OF TRAFFORD HOLDINGS LTD.
Trafford Catalogue #01-0253 www.trafford.com/robots/01-0253.html

10   9   8   7   6   5

SELLING POWER –
Marketing Energy Under Deregulation

We have used our best efforts to ensure the accuracy and reliability of information presented in this book. However, we make no warranty of any kind, expressed or implied, regarding the information contained herein.

Feedback, input and suggestions from interested parties are welcome.

Address correspondence to the authors at:

Drummond Consulting, Ltd.
6855 Jimmy Carter Boulevard,
Suite 2150
Norcross, Georgia 30071 USA

770.248.0210

www.drummondconsulting.net

ACKNOWLEDGMENTS

The authors wish to acknowledge the contributions of the following individuals without whose generous assistance and insight this book would not have been possible. Thanks also to those contributors in both Britain and the United States who have chosen to remain anonymous.

Mr. Warren Darby, President, Retail Energy Consultants, Inc., Mr. Frank Domurath, Call Center Professionals, Inc., Mr. Mark Goldman, President, 360, Inc., Dr. Jodi Monger, Customer Relationship Metrics and Mr. David Steele, Vice President, Marketing & Customer Services, Citizens Gas and Coke Utility.

Thanks also to our editor Susan Jensen who cleaned up much of Jim's "purple prose" and to Elise Drummond for giving valuable advice late in the process concerning the use of industry jargon and abbreviations. Your efforts are deeply appreciated.

CONTENTS

1. **Introduction**

2. **The Goals of Deregulation**

3. **Strategic Marketing Choices**
    Branding
    Advertising & Promotion
    Partnerships & Bundling

4. **Relationship Marketing/CRM**

5. **The Role of Customer Service**

6. **The Question of Outsourcing**

7. **Final Thoughts and Observations**

i. Endnotes
ii. List of resources and additional reading
iii. About the authors

Introduction

Energy providers face difficult choices as they work to develop marketing strategy in newly deregulated environments. Few products are more generic in the mind of consumers than basic utility services such as electricity and natural gas.

Under the previous scenario of controlled monopolies marketing efforts were primarily focused on pubic relations and retail sales. Most energy providers worked to insure positive public perception of the company through a combination of advertising and public service activities. A basic level of customer service was provided to whatever standard the utility chose to provide. Some companies also offered retail goods either through company run stores or through billing insert promotions.

These programs and strategies were appropriate to the time and in varying degrees were successful in accomplishing the stated objectives.

Marketing energy in a deregulated environment is an entirely different matter. With consumer choice comes the ability to change from one provider to another. The experience of companies in previously deregulated industries, such as long distance telephone service, gives clear evidence that historical dominance is no guarantee of future success. Customer loyalty is by no means a sure thing. New brands are introduced and capture significant market share, usually at the expense of the previous dominant player. Consumers have repeatedly shown that they will change suppliers for any number of reasons with price being but one of the factors prompting that change.

Given the technology and resources of 21st century business, competition may come, not only from established players in other markets but from those who want to enter the arena for reasons totally unrelated to selling energy. Tomorrow's competitor may well be a major supermarket chain, the local cable company, a discount retailer or a "generation X'er" with a laptop whose name we don't even know yet.

Old rules and practices do not bind new competitors. They perceive energy as just another product to add to their offerings and a tremendous opportunity to build a database of customers. Among the challenges faced by marketing executives preparing for open competition is to remain aware that the business will look very different tomorrow than it does today.

The strategic solution is to build the brand. That is, to develop significant market share and create customer retention programs that are so effective; customers will remain loyal regardless of enticements offered by new, unforeseen competitors.

What elements can the energy marketing professional utilize to maintain and increase share without product differentiation as a potential strategy? How can energy providers effectively and efficiently attract and retain customers over the long term while at the same time keeping marketing and service delivery costs at a minimum? Can smaller players compete with the growing strength of regional providers and newly created alliances between larger, better-financed energy conglomerates?

We will address these issues, suggest a new paradigm for the marketing professional and suggest strategies for succeeding in this new, highly competitive environment.

A Deregulation Proverb

"When the lion and the lamb lay down together it is better to be the lion."

THE GOALS OF DEREGULATION
✸

As the wave of conservative political thought swept through the United States in the late 1970's eventually leading to the election of Ronald Reagan in 1980, the deregulation of industries previously considered "untouchable" began in earnest. The tide became a ground swell, from the former president's deregulation of the airline industry to the court ordered divestiture of the Bell Telephone system from AT&T in 1984. At the state and local level like-minded legislators perceived that it was time to consider all potential targets; more specifically, electricity and natural gas.

In most cases, the stated long-term objective was to improve the efficiency of power generation and distribution while giving both residential and industrial consumers the opportunity to negotiate prices with their supplier of choice.

There were compelling arguments for this thinking. The experience of Great Britain, which under Margaret Thatcher privatized the nation's electricity industry in 1990, led to an overall 11% decline in domestic energy costs. Savings of over 1.6 billion British Pounds Sterling in the first five years of privatization made the United Kingdom's electric prices among the lowest in Europe. In 1998, at the start of total marketing deregulation, Britain's domestic prices for electricity were 27% less than Spain, 30% less than France and 33% less than Germany, including Value Added Tax (VAT).

In the United States, state or local regulatory authorities have historically set energy pricing. These governmental agencies are typically influenced by a variety of interest groups, each representing a different class of customer. Consumer advocates typically represent residential mass-market customers. That is their voice. Large industrial customers have both in-house energy management departments and also the ability to support lobbying efforts either directly or through trade associations. Mid-sized commercial customers, while using a significant amount of energy, are stuck in the middle. Consumer advocates do not represent them, nor do they have the political resources of large industrial users.

Manufacturing companies use a lot of energy. If national in scope they may have a plant in California, one in South Carolina and another in New York. It is understandable that this type of company finds it difficult to work in a system where energy costs vary so much from state to state. It is our belief that the genesis of most deregulation initiatives has been from this class of energy consumer. There is widespread belief among high volume customers that in the regulated environment they are, to some extent, subsidizing residential consumers.

Most of those in the industry to whom we have spoken believe that these large industrial customers have a point. This class of energy consumer, through their managers and lobbyists, often become strong advocates for deregulation. It stands to reason that at times, they may argue a position not necessarily consistent to what is in the best interest of the mass consumer. The conflicting agendas of large industrial users vs. mass market residential customers lies at the heart of the dilemma faced by legislators as they seek appropriate and workable solutions.

A second major issue for large volume energy customers is the opportunity to have open, direct access to the energy provider. If that were to happen, the possibility exists for a new supplier to come into the service territory and build a plant. In order to justify that expense the new generator must have the ability to get energy on the grid. They must have open access to the transmission system. This part of the process has actually been deregulated, in whole or in part, for many years.

In terms of mass marketing the issues are very similar for both electricity and natural gas providers. The progress of deregulation however has been quite different between the two. Overall there appears to be less incentive to wholly deregulate retail gas for the mass market. There are more inducements to unbundle or deregulate retail electricity. Demand is more consistent year-round for electricity than natural gas in most communities. Domestic migration statistics document a steady population shift to the Sunbelt states where natural gas consumption is minimal. If we factor in our aging Baby Boomer generation, it is likely that this trend will continue.

Simply stated, there is more money to be made, more consistently selling electricity to residential customers than natural gas. Electricity is consumed year-round while even in dual energy households many gas consumers are either heat-only or heat + hot water-only customers. We believe, given the finite nature of natural gas supply, that profit opportunities for those generating electricity are potentially greater than for gas on a long-term, nationwide basis.

Two states are currently at the forefront of the deregulation debate. California's effort to deregulate electricity, (what Time magazine described as "A crazy deregulation plan")[1] has become a feature of the nightly news. The state of Georgia deregulated natural gas in 1998 with decidedly mixed results. As of this writing 23 states have scheduled some form of electricity deregulation while 32 states, plus the District of Columbia, are at some phase of deregulating natural gas. The rest are taking a wait-and-see attitude towards the entire issue. The negative publicity generated by California's experience with deregulation has some elected officials rethinking their previous unconditional support for the concept.

A model or template of how to successfully accomplish deregulation of energy, provide open competition for all classes of customer and at the same time, insure consistent supply to meet demand is missing from the ongoing debate.

Also unclear is what becomes of those customers which providers elect not to serve. Those customers with poor payment histories or other characteristics considered "undesirable" are likely to be shunned by energy marketers. In Britain the issue is resolved by the installation of "Pay as you go" meters, a solution not likely to find acceptance in the United States. Legislators here may have to consider "energy pools", similar to what some states create for poor insurance risks, or some other formula for addressing what is certain to be a controversial side effect of total energy deregulation.

The model chosen for the state of Georgia is an anomaly. Atlanta Gas Light (AGL) the former sole supplier said in essence, "We want to run the infrastructure. We will have another division to deal with the retail end of it, but we just want to make money on pipes.". As a result AGL continues to operate as a traditional regulated monopoly but one that handles only distribution. Their belief is that as business expands there will be more pipes in the ground and AGL will thus earn a higher rate of return for the simple reason that they have a 100% share of that portion of the business.

AGL charges natural gas retailers a set monthly service fee which is then passed through to the consumer. Under this arrangement AGL enjoys the luxury of being segregated from the volatile cost of gas itself. The general public, faced with rising monthly bills, has put tremendous pressure on the Public Service Commission, (PSC) for pricing relief not only on the commodity but also on the set monthly fee. As of this writing the jury is still out on which classes of customers have actually benefited from Georgia's methodology for the deregulation of natural gas.

In an attempt to be fair to all providers who would be competing for residential business the Georgia PSC created a random allocation model. Consumers were given a specific time frame in which to choose an energy provider. At the end of the open enrollment period those customers who had not signed with a company were assigned one based upon the market share achieved to date. This had the obvious result of favoring those suppliers who had the deep pockets and/or marketing ability to gain market share quickly. Three companies dominated the early going: Georgia Natural Gas, the newly formed marketing arm of AGL, SCANA Energy and Shell Energy.[2]

From a marketing perspective the Georgia experience is a particularly interesting one. As mentioned earlier, the former monopoly supplier, Atlanta Gas Light Company, continues to operate the distribution system. AGL bills the marketer who in turn bills the customer. The marketer thus bears the risk of collection, not AGL. Consumers are placed in the somewhat confusing position of having one company sending them monthly bills for service while a different company is responsible for gas leak calls, new installations and meter reading. Energy marketers on the other hand are held accountable for a level of service quality that is effectively beyond their influence or control to any meaningful degree.

It has not been smooth sailing in Georgia. Consumers question the concept of "choice" since staying with the existing system and supplier was not one of the choices offered. Customers in states with pilot programs underway can often choose to participate in the new open pool of suppliers or remain with the existing regulated company.

Several Georgia marketers, unprepared for a large increase in call volume, strained to keep up with demands on customer service systems and billing procedures. By mid-1999 the Georgia PSC had received over

20,000 calls, primarily dealing with billing errors and poor customer service, primarily from irate citizens.

The number of natural gas marketers in Georgia has declined from 17 at the inception of open competition to eight today. The rest have either declared bankruptcy or departed the market having failed to achieve enough market share to support a viable, ongoing presence.

California's 1996 deregulation of the state's electricity industry attempted, in the words of the respected economist Robert J. Samuelson, to "...defy the law of supply and demand."[3]. The requirement that utilities sell their generating plants then purchase electricity from them combined with a freeze on retail prices proved a recipe for disaster. As of this writing Pacific Gas and Electric, one of the two largest energy providers in the state, has declared bankruptcy and the other, Southern California Edison is virtually insolvent.

Retail consumers have seen monthly bills increase not only because of the forced divestiture mentioned above but also due to an increase in the price of natural gas which powers many of California's generating plants. Governor Gray Davis concedes that electricity prices at the wholesale level in 2001 will increase at least 40% from 2000 levels. If one were to take a skeptical view of the entire California experience it might well include the idea that the state's legislators took a system that was not broken, and broke it.

The negative publicity surrounding California's energy issues and, to a lesser extent Georgia's experiment with natural gas deregulation, have had a measurable impact upon public perception. In an industry which once enjoyed highly favorable status among the general population a recent USA/CNN/Gallup Poll found only 28% of Americans continue to have confidence in the country's electric utilities.[4]

Our purpose in writing this book is not to debate the relative merits of deregulation. However, it would be less than candid not to acknowledge that the entire subject remains controversial. Energy providers are operating in a new and rapidly changing environment. Legislators and regulators will undoubtedly be influenced by the experiences, both positive and negative, of both Britain and those states who have attempted, with varying degrees of success, to accomplish the ultimate goals of deregulation.

Great Britain is used in some examples because the United Kingdom deregulated energy nationwide in 1998. We believe there are lessons to be learned from the British experience. We proceed state by state, municipality by municipality in the United States. Britain's government deregulated the entire country with the stroke of a pen and then made mid-course corrections as they became necessary and appropriate. We are able to observe what worked and what didn't in the UK and, hopefully, apply some of the lessons learned to our own emerging reality.

There remains a question as to the viability of comparing an island nation such as the United Kingdom with regulatory control resting at a central authority in London and the U.S. with 50 state and hundreds of local governments. In a worst case scenario we could be heading for a patchwork quilt of laws and regulations under which energy providers have to operate and compete. (Some have called this the Balkanization of energy policy.)

Clearly, no one in either the U.S. or Great Britain has found the perfect formula or created an ideal deregulation model for others to follow. The one thing we can state with a high degree of confidence is that the debate is likely to continue for some time to come.

Strategic Marketing Choices
✺

It is likely that no product or service is more generic in the mind of the average consumer than electricity or natural gas. Similar service industries receive much more subjective scrutiny. If a television picture becomes fuzzy the cable customer notices it. If a long distance supplier has consistent problems with connection speed or quality it is instantly evident. To the retail customer basic energy is either there or it is not. The lights either go on or they don't. The burners on the stove either work or they don't. The "product" is expected to be there. Our attention is aroused only when it is not. We cannot understate the difficult challenge facing the energy marketer charged with creating demand for a product that becomes notable only by its absence.

On the industrial side there is a "power quality" issue with electricity especially for those users with computers and other sophisticated equipment. The factory manager throws a switch and expects a steady, reliable flow of electricity to run his equipment. Any significant deviation can have serious consequences. On the natural gas side quality is measured in BTUs. Some burners have problems when gas companies must supplement the normal supply with liquefied natural gas (LNG) or propane/air on very cold days which can affect BTU levels.

While there are opportunities for segmentation of markets between commercial and industrial users of both types of energy, differentiation of the product itself at the residential, mass market level is virtually impossible.

Marketing approaches as taught in business schools have historically been based around the concept of "The Four P's." Those being; product, price, placement and promotion. While price and promotion remain options for energy marketers, product and placement are a given.

Energy marketers are at a disadvantage, even when compared with non-utility service industries. For example, a customer might choose one airline over another due to a more convenient scheduled departure (place) or some combination of more comfortable seats, better food or a perceived level of service (product). It is worth repeating that of the challenges facing the energy marketing professional, the most daunting is the reality that product and placement are a given. We must look elsewhere to find strategies that will insure long-term success and profitability.

A company's marketing efforts in traditional regulated environments was a narrowly focused activity due in part to the reality of the business. Generally speaking this historical reality:

- Assumes a captive customer base
- Has no perceived price/benefit ratio
- Has limited advertising & branding initiatives
- Is perceived as "background music" by consumers
- Offers retail goods that lack price/value relationship
- Has questionable customer loyalty, having never been challenged

Energy providers in the deregulated environment can expect fierce competition for each and every customer. Their brand must be well recognized, service quality must be of a high standard, customer loyalty must be constantly nurtured and retail goods perceived as having a high price/value relationship when compared to those offered in general retail distribution.

The marketing professional in the deregulated environment must overcome many obstacles not the least of which are:

- Traditional advertising and promotional activities
- The lack of connection between marketing and customer service
- Corporate inertia – an unwillingness to adapt and change

As current energy providers make plans for the change to an open, competitive environment and new entrants prepare to enter the market, senior decision makers must understand the holistic nature of the marketing process. With that understanding comes the knowledge that the organization's operations, at every functional level, have a profound effect on the ultimate outcome of the marketing effort.

Regrettably, it is not uncommon for senior executives to perceive marketing as an activity, not a strategy; as an event, not a process. In truth, marketing encompasses every aspect of the company's operation that in a multitude of ways affects inter-relationships with customers. In our view, marketing begins with the very first exposure a consumer has to the company and continues through to insuring ongoing customer satisfaction and long-term relationship building. It is a process without end.

It is all too common for a company to devise a "marketing plan" which is in reality an advertising campaign. Consider the difference. Peter Mayle, defines a campaign as, "A collection of advertisements…spread across TV, press, posters and radio, which are in theory expressing the same advertising message (the campaign theme) in a variety of ways."[5]

Marketing on the other hand, when done properly and effectively, is the sum total of all factors which bring goods and services to the attention of potential customers, creates desire and reinforces the purchasing decision once it is made. **Marketing is the central, strategic plan that determines the ultimate success or failure of the enterprise.**

We recently worked with a major international corporation who needed help bringing a new product to market. They had spent millions in development and built a new factory to produce it. They were convinced that by the very act of creation and production, customers would come to them and purchase the item. When we took on the assignment warehouses were bursting with over a one year supply. Senior management was sincerely bewildered at the product's "failure" to sell.

The scenario is all too common. This company had a *production plan*, not a marketing plan. Management forgot the simplest rule of all; you make money only by *selling* a product, not producing it. You can build it, but seldom will customers beat a path to your door. Somewhere along the line you must create a compelling reason for someone to act. Customers must be persuaded to change their current behavior and try something new. In business-to-business transactions overcoming the built-in inertia of buyers is probably more difficult than altering the purchasing habits of retail end-users. In either case, the challenge is the same. You must create a compelling argument for change.

What tools can the energy marketer utilize to attract and retain customers with this broad concept of marketing in mind? The following four elements have proven to be successful for energy marketers and should form the basis of your strategic plan.

- Branding and image building – developing top-of-mind awareness with both current and prospective customers

- Effective price/value positioning – the company must be perceived as being competitive, while not necessarily the least expensive, compared with offerings from others

- Aggressive customer relationship management – the ability to gain competitive advantage by providing exceptional customer service can be a powerful tool for both attraction and retention

- Partnering and bundling of products and services – using the extensive data base profile of existing customers to expand product offerings

Experience to date indicates that suppliers who have effectively implemented some combination of these strategies are winning the battle for customers. On the other hand, those who have attempted to compete in the arena of open competition using older, more traditional approaches have for the most part either retreated from the market or been absorbed by larger, more successful competitors.

We question the viability of the traditional marketing model in today's fast-paced, connected world as we begin to look at alternatives to past methods. Not that the "Four P's" are any less necessary, the question is, do they go far enough?

The price issue is one example. There are those who argue that energy, given its generic nature, is a price driven commodity. It is important to recognize that residential customers are motivated by a complex blend of attitudes and perceptions of which price is but one factor, unlike business-to-business industrial customers to whom price is undoubtedly a principal driver.

Obviously, a given suppliers price per therm or kilowatt-hour cannot be so out of line with competition that it becomes an issue unto itself. The important factor is Perceived Value which might expressed as:

Perceived service level ÷ price = Perceived Value

Research is required in each individual market to determine the extent to which customers will change suppliers at what level of price differentiation. On a national basis, most existing data suggests that a "very satisfied" customer will not change suppliers until the price per unit is at least ten percent higher than what competitors are charging.

It is also important for the energy marketer to establish for his or her specific demographic area which customers will be sought after and nurtured and which will be merely accepted. This represents a significant change from the days of regulation in which all customers were accepted and the challenge became how to deal with those less credit worthy or otherwise less desirable to the provider.

Customers considered "desirable" are those who consume an amount of energy consistent with their location, family size and lifestyle. In addition, desirable customers are those who pay their bills in a timely manner and remain with a vendor over the long term thus maximizing return on investment (ROI) at the micro level.

Informed marketers in many industries have created systems for tracking customer lifetime value (CLV). These enlightened professionals have come to realize that attracting customers is but one step in an ongoing process of capture, retention and enhancement. This idea of developing and nurturing exchange relationships between customer and supplier over time is sometimes referred to as "Relationship Marketing".

More recently, especially among energy providers, the new buzzword is "Customer Relationship Management" (CRM).

It is undoubtedly true that CRM is a valuable tool for building customer loyalty and increasing customer lifetime value. The caveat is that CRM applies primarily to existing customers. CRM alone does not solve the challenge of attracting new customers except when leveraged as part of an overall marketing strategy.

In the next section we will present some ideas and strategies that the energy marketer may wish to consider as he or she prepares for the deregulated future. This is by necessity a work in progress due to the very nature of the subject and the ever-changing reality of the business. Our goal is to provide a toolbox of ideas that may be of value in designing your marketing plan. We hope you will find the information informative, interesting and perhaps challenging to accepted notions. We encourage you to think "way outside the box" and develop a strategy appropriate to your own company's specific goals and corporate culture.

Branding

A brand must be more than just a logo or slogan in order to be effective. Your brand must stand for something, mean something and inspire a positive reaction in everyone who encounters it. (Sometimes referred to as "brand essence".) Your brand is a dynamic representation of all that your company says and does. It is a visual representation of the promise you make to customers every single day. Over the long-term consumers reward brands which deliver on that promise.

Federal Express has a powerful promise, "When it absolutely, positively must be there overnight.". The ability of FedEx to consistently deliver on that promise has made them one of the most successful package delivery services in the world. L.L. Bean, the Maine based retailer of clothing and sporting goods, is another example. Customers buy with confidence in the knowledge that since 1912, L.L. Bean has promised and delivered on their ironclad guarantee of satisfaction, regardless of how long the customer owns the product.

An energy supplier, to be a viable competitor in the deregulated environment, must have a clear, easy-to-understand brand identity which customers recognize, remember and form a positive association. Consumers at all levels inherently wish to do business with companies they know and respect. The energy supplier's brand, and associated visual image (or logo) must convey a clear message of reliability, stability and accessibility.

The development of an easy-to-understand identity that potential customers both remember and associate themselves with is among the most powerful tools available to the marketing professional.

Webster's New World Dictionary defines *brand* as, "A stick that is burning" from the base word, *burn* as in "burned into an object, person or thing". The Oxford English Dictionary dates the word to the Middle Ages. Thus, the phrase *"Brand New"* literally means, "new from the fire". In other words, a brand is something that leaves a lasting imprint or impression.

The trick is to insure that the lasting impression is a positive one. Once tarnished it is exceedingly difficult to rebuild your brand among the general public. The general public being comprised of individuals who make buying decisions on a highly personal basis. As marketers we tend to put large groups of people into categories and refer to them as "the market" or "the target market" and so forth. It is important to remember that successful marketing requires hundreds or thousands of ***individual buying decisions made one at a time, one person at a time.***

It is an old cliché that states, "You are only as good as your good name.". This is as true in today's fast-paced, technology driven world as it was in frontier times. ***A brand represents who and what you are. It is a promise, a statement about what a customer can expect when choosing to do business with you.***

We especially enjoy the analogy offered by Harriet Rubin. To paraphrase her comments; Federal Express is a *promise*. The U.S. Postal Service on the other hand is a *prediction*, "We'll deliver it to the address shown, (hopefully) at some undefined time in the future."[6]. Quite a difference.

The Nike swoosh logo is a promise of well-designed athletic footwear. Starbucks is a promise of premium coffee served in a pleasant, friendly atmosphere. Wal-Mart offers the promise of good quality merchandise at, "Always the lowest price, always.". BMW is, "The Ultimate Driving Machine". You can think of dozens of examples to support the point. The perception potential customers have of your brand has a profound impact in their decision making process.

Southwest Airlines stands out as an example of successful branding in service industries. Southwest has carved out a profitable niche for itself with low fares, limited amenities and reliable day-to-day service against major competition from far larger players. As a company, they consistently follow one of the basic rules of customer interaction: under-promise and over-deliver.

Marketers all too often confuse branding with image. They are two very different things. An image can be thought of as a static thing; a sign, a symbol or an idea. A successful brand on the other hand evokes a feeling. It connects with the heart, not just the head. Human motivation is not often a rational thing. Consumer behavior is seldom a well-defined reaction to an intellectual evaluation of all available choices. It is more often an emotional reaction to a product's story than to the product itself.

Every year thousands of people drive to Spring Hill, Tennessee to visit the place where Saturn cars are produced. Now few would seriously argue that Saturn is a high tech, state-of-the art representation of automotive excellence. And yet their owners are among the most loyal in the land. Satisfaction levels, as measured by J.D. Power & Associates, rank among the top five automobile brands alongside such stalwarts as Lexus and Mercedes Benz. Saturn has created a brand that through their advertising, dealer service, sales training and ongoing customer interaction program has encouraged customers to consider themselves part of a family. It is a family of happy, content, enthusiastic owners who share the common bond of driving a vehicle produced in a small Tennessee town, just for them. Oldsmobile's marketing should have been so successful.

We believe an essential ingredient of a successful energy marketing strategy is the creation and promotion of a positive corporate image. The corporate brand and logo must convey a positive message of stability, reliability and exceptional service. Customer choice in the deregulated environment is driven by the perception of your company vs. competition. Effective brand development is the first step in that process.

This concept comes with a caveat. Branding alone cannot insure success. To be effective, the brand image created must be an accurate representation of both the corporate culture and the reality of customer experience.

Referring back to our earlier example, consider the reaction if the United States Postal Service adopted the slogan, "We will get it there overnight, guaranteed"? Would anyone believe it? Would credibility rise or fall? Remember, "Neither rain, nor sleet nor snow nor dark of night shall stay this carrier from his appointed rounds!"? Little perceived credibility in that slogan either. It would be far better and more effective if the Postal Service promoted the reality of their offering. Let's say that, hypothetically, they changed their slogan to: "We are dedicated to delivering mail to each and every address in the United States in a reasonable amount of time for the lowest possible cost."

That makes sense. Customers know there are faster services but also know there are higher costs involved. The Postal Service's theoretical campaign builds credibility by promoting what they do well, that is, delivering correspondence without a sense of urgency to every address, and doing it inexpensively.

There are many successful brands among energy providers and some not so successful. Two good examples of branding well done are Centrica (formerly British Gas) in the UK and SCANA Energy in the U.S.

SCANA is a virtual case study in how an aggressive branding approach can result in the acquisition of a large number of customers against formidable competition. Warren Darby, SCANA's Senior Vice President at the time of their entry into the Georgia marketplace said,

"When the decision was made to expand our reach beyond South Carolina to the state of Georgia we began by conducting marketing research to determine how familiar Georgians were with our company. We did this in both Atlanta and Augusta, Georgia. Augusta was chosen since it is on the border with South Carolina. As a South Carolina based company we assumed Augusta residents would be more familiar with us.".

Darby continues, "We were wrong. The SCANA name not only failed to register with survey respondents, the fictitious name we created as a control, Delta Gas Light, achieved a five percent brand recognition, well ahead of our own one percent!"[7]

Significantly, despite his nearly 30 years in the business, Darby and his team realized that traditional marketing approaches were not likely to achieve the results senior management desired. This was reflected in their choice of an advertising agency to bring SCANA's message to the general population.

"After a lot of internal discussion we decided to eliminate any agency that had previously worked with a utility." Darby said. "We narrowed our choices down to three finalists and picked the one that presented the most aggressive campaign. We were especially impressed that the agency head, Joel Babbit of 360, Inc., was prepared to walk away from the account if we were not willing to approach the market in a very specific manner. Joel told us, 'Make no mistake. If you choose us we are going to advertise SCANA as if we were selling Ginsu Steak Knives. We are going to treat you as a consumer product and promote you accordingly. With all the companies coming into this state to compete for market share the only way to succeed is to develop a strong message and tell it often.'"

According to Mark Goldman, 360's President, "We developed a focused, in-your-face marketing campaign. It was clear from the beginning that we had to both establish the SCANA brand as a reliable, local provider and also provide a sense of urgency on the part of the consumer to respond immediately. We knew we had to level the playing field and establish SCANA as a credible company involved with the community. Even before open competition began we were sponsoring picnics around the state to promote the SCANA brand name. To overcome our lack of physical visibility in the state, we partnered with Kroger Supermarkets by placing kiosks in 32 of their 50 Georgia locations."8

The success of this approach is obvious from figure 1. When competition for consumer business began in 1999 SCANA's unaided brand awareness had increased from virtually nothing, (remember Delta Gas Light?) to the most recognized name in Georgia. SCANA scored even higher than the newly created Georgia Natural Gas Services, a spin-off from the former monopoly supplier, Atlanta Gas Light Company.

Figure 1

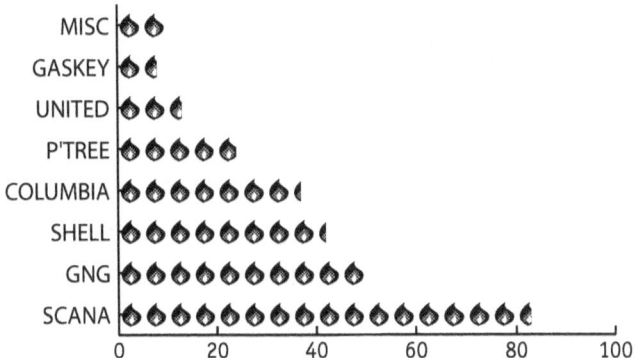

"Our goal" Mark Goldman said, "was to achieve a 10% market share for SCANA the first six months they did business in Georgia. In fact, at the end of six months we were three years ahead of plan! Put another way, SCANA signed up more new customers the first six months of operation in Georgia than they had developed over 150 years operating in South Carolina.".

In addition to signing up thousands of residential customers in the early days of open competition, SCANA's efforts were recognized by industry observers as one of the most successful marketing campaigns ever conducted in the business. Dave Altman, Vice President of The Southern Company was quoted in The Wall Street Journal as saying, *"SCANA has built a brand from nothing in five months. I don't think anyone thought that could happen."*.[9]

In the United Kingdom, British Gas (BG) was a holdover from the former government owned monopoly, privatized since The First Gas Act of 1986. While widely known among the British public, the kindest thing you could say was that positive brand recognition and customer loyalty was less than enthusiastic.

In 1996 with the reality of open retail competition less than a year away, the infrastructure, (or "pipes") portion of BG was separated from the retail consumer side. Company executives created an entirely new name identity, Centrica. The new name was introduced in an aggressive advertising and promotional campaign with little mention of its connection with the former British Gas. The re-branding effort was an unqualified success. As of this writing, Centrica enjoys the highest market share among UK natural gas providers, currently estimated at over 70%. This is truly a remarkable figure when you consider that the highest market share attained by any of the UK's electricity providers is less than 15%.

Clearly, an emphasis on brand identity is a critical factor to successfully competing in an open market environment. A brand can be a company's most valuable and yet most fragile asset. Your brand represents the entire sum of experience consumers have with your company. It is something to be diligently nurtured and protected.

Developing a theme and an identity that accurately represents the company's core values and corporate culture is the beginning of the branding process. Contrary to the thinking that goes into many such efforts, designing a new logo and using it as part of an advertising campaign is not branding. Effective branding is a far more complex process. In the early stages, you are making a promise to those with whom you hope to do business. The extent to which the company delivers on that promise will, to a large extent, determine market share growth and ultimately, the success or failure of the enterprise.

ADVERTISING AND PROMOTION

If we begin with the premise that a successful marketing program contains some degree of ongoing interaction between buyers and sellers, (figure 2.) then our initial goal must be to create desire in the mind of the consumer to select one provider over another.

There must be a shift in thinking to the realization that the company and its services are now a PRODUCT. A product to be advertised, promoted and sold like any other.

Figure 2

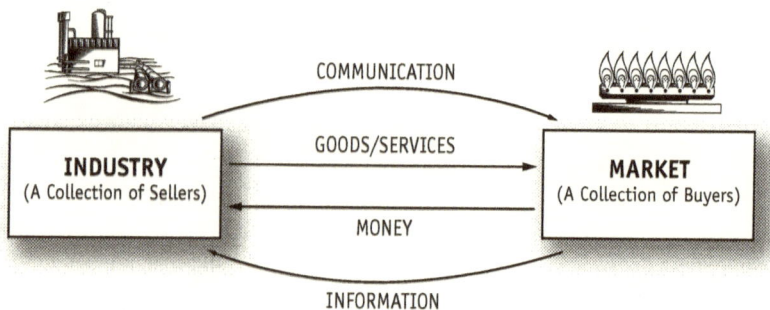

It bears repeating a point made earlier. Customer choice in service industries, such as energy, is based upon the *perception of a given company vs. competition*. As professional marketing people we must always keep this critical fact in mind. Consumers do not necessarily make choices based upon all available facts and statistics. By and large they make purchasing decisions based upon their *perception of reality*, not reality itself. Perception that is based upon several obvious and not-so-obvious factors including:

- Price
- Commitment
- Company values
- Reliability of service
- Third party endorsements or recommendations

Returning to our example of SCANA's entry into the state of Georgia, 360's Mark Goldman states that a combination of key ingredients led to their success. "It's a three legged stool." Goldman said, "You must be visible in the marketplace. We call that real estate. Media selection and direct response advertising are essential. The affinity group campaign, (described elsewhere) was incredibly successful and brought thousands of new customers to the company."

It is tempting to believe that price is the determining factor in customer choice. However, studies of consumer behavior have consistently shown that most customers will not change supplier solely to obtain a lower price. In fact only nine percent of surveyed customers changed for that reason. 14% changed due to dissatisfaction with perceived quality. The vast majority, over two thirds, changed due to, "indifference on the part of their supplier".[10]

Those who make the mistake of believing that price is the primary motivator do so at their peril. First, because price alone is seldom a determinant. If a company is perceived as having the lowest price but not committed to the business, is a major polluter or has bad word-of-mouth among the general public, that supplier is unlikely to build a satisfactory base of customers. Second, an energy supplier whose customer base is comprised primarily of customers motivated by price alone will over time undoubtedly find they have attracted a clientele that are the least loyal and least desirable for long term success. Simply put, if they came to you for price they will likely leave you for the same reason. If systems are in place to track CLV, the price-only customer comes out at the low end of the equation.

Conversely, the customer attracted to a brand due to perceived quality of service and an ongoing commitment to them personally will seldom change suppliers until a price difference becomes significant enough to warrant attention.

One challenge facing all advertisers is finding a way to break through the massive quantity of messages which daily bombard customers both in print and over the airwaves. It is estimated that the average male in the United States sees over 30,000 television commercials per year. 30,000! Add to that figure the number of 30 second spots heard on radio, the thousands of ads that appear on computer screens, the volume of direct mail and the visual influence of billboards. That is a lot of clutter.

Successful consumer advertising, including that of energy providers, must have a "call to action", a specific reason for the potential customer to respond to the message. The generic, image-oriented advertising of the past while viable for building brand credibility is not likely to generate immediate response. In the deregulated environment, response is exactly what you are looking for. No matter how powerful the branding or image creation effort each and every advertisement ideally contains elements that promote a sense of urgency to "act now".

SCANA Energy did a particularly good job implementing this concept in the early stages of their Georgia campaign. Advertising agency president Mark Goldman working with SCANA's Warren Darby created a strategy totally focused on generating customer response. An early promotion offered the choice of $ 50.00 in free gas or a $ 50.00 supermarket gift certificate. Customer acquisitions were tracked weekly and reported monthly. Adjustments in advertising placement were made based upon analysis of which ads and what media were producing the best results.

Especially successful was a program wherein local charities, schools and affinity groups received $ 50.00 contributions for each of their members who signed with SCANA as their natural gas supplier. "The response to our charitable institution campaign was incredible." said Warren Darby. "From local churches and schools to Boy Scout troops and amateur sports organizations we had nearly one hundred non-profit groups sending letters to their members, on their own letterheads, urging them to choose SCANA. This represented a strong endorsement of our company from a known and trusted source. We gave thousands to various charities in Georgia through this program. It really was a win/win scenario for everyone."

It is important to consider that we are fighting for attention, not only with direct competitors but with all other consumer–oriented advertising as well when developing a strategy to attract new customers. A successful campaign breaks through the clutter and prompts immediate action on the part of the customer.

Equally important is to remain aware of the tendency among many advertising agencies to create campaigns with great visceral appeal to the client and/or public but which do little to promote customer response. (In industry jargon, "Art above action") Our own anecdotal experience validates this point. How may times have you or a friend seen a particularly clever advertisement and commented, "That was great! What were they selling?"

An effective campaign to win customers, especially in the early months of open competition, generates a sense of immediacy. The goal at this stage is to attract new customers either by direct response to a customer call center or with a visit to a retail location. We believe, at the risk of offending some in the creative community, that it matters little if potential customers "like" the ads or even remember them. ***The only thing that matters is the number of people who actually respond and apply for service.***

Media selection is obviously an important factor. The mix of television, radio, newspaper, direct mail and outdoor must be carefully evaluated. Generally speaking, television has proven the most effective medium in producing immediate response with radio a close second. It is unfortunate, but true nonetheless, that in many cities fewer than 30% of the local population reads a daily newspaper. Likewise, direct mail has proven of limited use even when coupons or other incentives are included.

Personal visits to customer homes have been highly successful in parts of the UK but much less so in the U.S. The reason for this difference is primarily cultural. In Britain house-to-house direct marketing is perceived as a positive, personal experience while Americans tend to be suspicious of door-to-door solicitations of any kind.

Spot television accounted for nearly 40% of the total media buy in the early days of SCANA's entry into the Georgia market. Radio accounted for another third of the budget with local disc jockeys and other on-air personalities giving personal endorsements for the company's service. The balance of the advertising budget was spent with local newspapers and to implement the affinity program with local charities.

According to Warren Darby, "Our original goal was to acquire 150,000 customers. We ended up getting over 400,000! The initial campaign was far more successful than expected."

Interestingly, SCANA chose to shun telemarketing completely. Research by their agency, 360, Inc., determined that the general public had become increasingly negative to telephone solicitations. To emphasize the point, SCANA even offered to pay the five dollars necessary to put customers on a "no call" list maintained and enforced by the state of Georgia. The approach was incorporated into SCANA's advertising campaign with the slogan; "No contracts. No telemarketing. No kidding!"

If outbound telemarketing is considered a negative, effective *inbound* service is essential. All the advertising in the world is money wasted if the customer calls to apply for service and is unable to reach a representative in a reasonable period of time. People will remain on hold when you are the only game in town. With multiple choices available customers will seldom wait more than a few minutes. Ironically, your advertising may have done its job and the customer is now "in the market" for an energy supplier. If they cannot reach you, they will likely call your competitors until they find one who answers promptly and courteously.

In a regulated environment call centers are typically open 10-12 hours a day, five days a week, except for emergency calls. With open competition comes the necessity to be available 24/7, a big change.

Marketing professionals are well advised to consider current demographic research in creating strategy. It is quite remarkable how many businesses continue to operate as if we were still living in an "Ozzie & Harriet" or "Father Knows Best" environment in which the husband goes off to work while the wife stays home to keep house and wait for the repairman to show up. According to the most recent census less than 30 percent of American households fit that idealized model. Increasingly, family units are comprised of single parent families or those with both adults working outside the home. Inherently, we know this new reality has changed the very fabric of our society and the way business is conducted. Yet a surprising number of companies continue to ignore these trends and operate as if it were still the 1950's. The true professional adapts his or her processes and systems to serve customers when and where necessary.

It is also tempting to direct potential customers to a web site on the Internet. In practice this strategy has failed to produce significant results. For whatever reason customers in the early stages of open competition have shown a strong preference to either phone a call center or sign up in-person at a company store or kiosk.

Partnerships and Bundling

We have already mentioned the power of third party endorsements by charitable organizations. Business partnerships can be equally effective.

SCANA Energy partnered with both Delta Airlines and Kroger Supermarkets. Following the initial $ 50.00 per new customer campaign, SCANA switched to giving mileage credits in Delta's frequent flyer program. Their partnership with Kroger included placing kiosks in strategically located stores where customers could sign on and immediately receive a gift certificate for that day's shopping.

While the incentives were undoubtedly a motivator the very fact that recognized and trusted names such as Delta and Kroger were partnering with SCANA created both credibility and confidence to choose a previously unknown supplier over competition.

Membership cooperatives are another valuable source of partnerships. In Georgia, SCANA aggressively sought to join forces with local electric co-ops to bundle natural gas with other services. Cobb EMC, one of the nation's largest electric cooperatives serving the fast growing suburbs north of Atlanta, was an early success story. Cobb's CEO, Dwight Brown, had long recognized the need to add additional service offerings and SCANA's natural gas was an ideal fit. Several other regional co-ops also joined SCANA and together provided thousands of new customers. The opportunities for bundling of services and joint billing can make this type of partnership beneficial to both parties.

Ironically, when proposed in Britain, the national regulator at first opposed the bundling of services and for a brief time required electronic "firewalls" between data bases to prevent energy suppliers from leveraging this valuable resource. It did not take long for the providers themselves to point out that this action effectively contradicted the very spirit of open competition and within months the firewall regulation was rescinded.

Several British energy marketers have experimented with bundling services including; telephone, cable television, gas with electricity and vice versa. Perhaps the most successful of these efforts has been Centrica's Goldfish MasterCard. You can get an overview of their program by viewing the Goldfish website at www.goldfishguide.com. Scottish & Southern Energy sells both electricity and natural gas and partners with Argos, a nationwide catalog showroom, to offer retail consumer goods.

We have received feedback from some energy company executives that one unified bill for a variety of services brings with it a degree of risk. "It's bad enough," one manager said, "that we have to justify a higher gas bill than the customer expected. When they get a massive bill that includes electricity, cable TV and security service they (the customer) finds it hard to differentiate between them all. They are faced with one large bill instead of several smaller ones. For us at least, the idea did not work."

With that caveat in mind the concept of bundling services with combined, one-source billing remains an attractive one. In addition to electricity and natural gas there are obvious additions such as cable television, home security and telephone service. Perhaps not so obvious is the possibility to provide service contracts for household appliances and affinity credit cards.

Relationship Marketing/CRM

❋

While there are probably as many definitions of "Relationship Marketing" as there are writers on the subject, Christian Gronroos in his seminal work on the subject, "Managing the Moments of Truth in Service Competition" gives one both succinct and comprehensive.

"Relationship marketing is to identify, establish, maintain and enhance relationships with customers at a profit so that the objectives of all parties are met." [11]

The concept of Customer Relationship Management, or CRM is highly visible in management literature today. For our purposes, it doesn't matter if we call it relationship marketing or CRM; the basic concept is the same. It is the practice of utilizing data base management tools to enhance the customer's relationship with the company and build upon that good will to establish customer lifetime value, create positive word-of-mouth endorsements and pursue opportunities for additional business.

This is hardly a new idea. At its core, relationship marketing (or CRM) is actually a return to the basics of facilitating exchanges between buyer and seller. An exchange process that likely can be traced back to the first instance of our distant ancestors exchanging meat from a recent kill for a spark of fire. In more recent times commerce was conducted between merchants who knew their customers' names, preferences and buying habits and customized their products and services on a highly individual basis.

Advances in digital storage and retrieval provide the ability to catalog vast amounts of data. We can now track customer attitudes, behaviors, likes and dislikes using technology that didn't exist 20 years ago. Sophisticated software applications allow us to provide highly individualized service to thousands of customers in real time, all the time.

Writing in the Financial Times, Peter Martin's article, "The Death of Geography" includes the statement, "..the combination of telecommunications, computing power and ever more discriminating customers – trends which are individually unremarkable – are producing a profound change in the relationship between companies and their customers."[12]

While the mom-and-pop grocery store down the street is a distant memory, modern computer systems make it possible to apply personalization on a global basis. We do not have to look far to find companies who have utilized this practice to competitive advantage. How else, with their millions of customers, can the operator at L.L. Bean ask how I am enjoying the fly rod I purchased last fall and if the sleeping bags proved warm enough? This is using technology to provide personal service of a level designed to produce long-term loyalty, and it does.

L.L. Bean has some of the most sophisticated relationship marketing tools in existence. Every operator in their 24/7 call center has access to a wealth of information about their customers and the authority to solve problems whenever they occur.

It is the dealership and customer service experience that separates Saturn cars from their many competitors, not the product itself. Dealer salespeople are trained to be information specialists with the goal of making the entire buying experience as painless and fear-free as possible. Saturn's customer service personnel are empowered to go the extra mile up to and including offering a replacement vehicle if the situation warrants.

Saturn uses what they call a, "One-call resolution strategy". Customer service personnel have an information data-base that allows them to answer virtually all questions and concerns voiced by callers. By adding three-way calling capability Saturn's staff can link the customer directly to a dealer service person and work towards a resolution. In the process of implementing the "One-call" strategy, Saturn's managers learned one of CRM's most powerful lessons. **People who have problems and get them resolved are much more likely become repeat customers than those who never had a problem at all.** In Saturn's case this has translated into an 80% retention rate.

Conversely, a major player in the deregulated long distance business, (whose familiar name our attorney will not let us print here) exhibited great expertise at attracting new customers in the early days of competitive long distance while failing spectacularly to retain them. We don't want to single this company out individually but rather use them as just one example of a common truth. That truth being the tendency to spend a majority of the company's resources on attraction and little if any on retention.

There is strong evidence that the traditional "Four P's" marketing model is increasingly incompatible with changes in consumer demographics, behavior and lifestyle. With those changes has come an increasing reliance upon new and evolving mediums of communication to develop long-term relationships between customers and firms selling both products and services.

When speaking to groups of marketing professionals, we often ask the question, "What percentage of your current marketing budget is dedicated to retention?" In those few instances where any response is forthcoming it is usually, "Well, that's not our department's responsibility." or something similar.

Playing devil's advocate one has to ask, if it is not the marketing department's responsibility to keep all these new customers being attracted by the promotional budget, then whose is it? Who is making the decision to spend millions on an advertising campaign while spending virtually nothing to insure that new customers attracted by that campaign are satisfied?

Harvard professor Frederick Reichheld's excellent book on the subject, *"The Loyalty Effect"* indicates that retaining just five percent more of a company's existing customer base can boost the value of an average customer by 25 to 100 percent. 100% ! Taking one real-world company as an example Reichheld found, "In the 90-percent retention scenario…earnings grow very slowly to $ 96 million at the end of ten years. With 95-percent retention earnings grow almost 50-percent faster, to $ 141 million."[13]

You would think that with this strong evidence of the positive benefits to the bottom line service industries such as energy providers would be falling all over themselves to build customer loyalty. But as Reichheld points out, financial managers and financially oriented CEO's are often the number one enemy of customer loyalty.

*"…generally accepted accounting practices actually **hide** the value of a loyal customer, an impressive feat of concealment given what loyalty can do for the great majority of companies."*[14]

Customer satisfaction is often considered the exclusive domain of the customer service department in the consumer electronics industry, as in many others. In the real world that translates into fixing broken products and, at times, arguing over whom is to pay for the repair. Most companies in this industry build very high quality, innovative products. Yet in those instances where problems do occur, customers are often lost forever due to an inability on the part of the manufacturer to handle complaints and problems in a mutually satisfactory manner. There are clearly defined procedures for repairing *products*. Not so clear is where the responsibility rests for repairing broken customer *relationships*.

CRM recognizes the fact that building customer relationships is more than just fixing a problem or making the customer complaint go away. Properly planned and implemented, an effective CRM strategy not only builds customer loyalty but also provides the company with an invaluable data base of information that management can utilize to make their product or service more attractive to potential customers.

One reason for the internal disconnection between marketing and service comes from the historic separation of traditional roles. The process of creating and implementing marketing strategies, especially when products fly off the shelves, is an exciting one. Taking care of problems after the sale, including dealing with the occasional irate customer, is anything but a fun experience! However when quality scores begin declining among both customers and dealers, it becomes more and more difficult to build long-term repeat business.

Most research on the subject indicates that for every customer who openly complains, 20 or more had the same experience but never told the company about it. This same "silent" customer does however tell an average 10-15 of his or her friends while taking future business elsewhere.

The banking industry is a good service-oriented example. It is no secret that with mergers and acquisitions we are rapidly moving towards the day when a few major players will dominate banking in the United States, similar to what has already occurred in the airline industry. Recently, we had the experience of pulling 100% of our business away from a major financial institution due to continuing errors and indifferent customer service. During the entire process of closing the accounts, not one person asked why we were changing banks. There was no established procedure or questionnaire to determine why they had lost us as a customer. Were we moving out of the area? Did we receive a better offer elsewhere? Did we respond to a competitor's advertising campaign? Were we dissatisfied with their level of service? They will never know for the simple reason that they never asked.

This company's annual advertising budget is in the millions of dollars. Millions. And yet, it is obvious that very little is being invested in providing exceptional customer service and virtually nothing devoted to an ongoing customer retention strategy.

This is bad business practice by any measure. If we use Dr. Jon Anton's figure that it is 30% more efficient to retain an existing customer than obtain a new one[15] who at this bank is tracking customers gained vs. customers lost and why? Who is answering to the stockholders for this gross inefficiency? This company could learn volumes about their perceived level of service with the minuscule investment in an exit questionnaire for departing customers. With this invaluable database of information they could strategize effective customer retention initiatives in support of their desired growth and profit objectives. For whatever reason, they choose not to do so.

When Fred Hanna was Vice President of SCANA Energy his customer service team actively tracked down complaints. Complaints were seen as an opportunity to build customer loyalty and gather information on internal processes in need of improvement, rather than viewing them as a problem.

The big "AHA", in utilities involves questions around billing. The customer that says, "I got my bill and there is no way I used that much energy." This gets right to the marketing issue of perception vs. reality. In truth, the meter itself almost never mis-registers. They are better than 99.999 percent accurate. If you have confidence in the accuracy of those physically reading the meters, customer service personnel can respond with a high degree of authority. On the other hand if your meter reading is only 98% accurate, the possibility exists for 200 customers out of every 10,000 to be requesting a repeat reading. In this scenario, you have just gone from a $ 3.00 phone call to a $ 30.00 cost for sending a truck and meter reader out to the customer's home, a ten-to-one increase. If the second reading fails to resolve the issue, a meter test is required. That's a $ 300.00 cost. It does not take a CPA to determine the efficiency of resolving this type of complaint during the first customer contact if at all possible.

The bottom line is that the more effective you can manage your processes, the fewer complaints and the higher the company's profits. Yet, in most energy companies the customer service function is still considered a cost center, not a potential profit center.

CRM is a philosophy of marketing that looks at the process from a service prospective rather than a sales prospective. It advances the idea that marketing must be built on relationships rather than transactions. The growing importance of customer retention, the advent of the global economy and increasing recognition of customer relationship economics are making the traditional marketing mix a very narrow one indeed.

Two popular management texts, *"The One to One Future"* in the US and, *"Relationship Marketing"* in the UK both espouse similar theories. In essence, they contend that marketing in the new millennium will increasingly depend upon strategic planning which includes traditional customer service functions and quality issues as part of the overall marketing mix.

Why this idea often falls on deaf ears is understandable. First, if it is adopted, the role of the marketing professional is elevated to a level never before achieved in most companies. Second, it requires that each and every department in the organization must be responsible for its part in supporting the overall strategic plan. And third, it's just plain hard work.

The skill set of tomorrow's marketing professional will cut across virtually all functional areas. The head of marketing will no longer be seen as solely a creative role, but will be responsible for every aspect of customer contact, attraction and retention.

Finally, in the flurry of activity by hardware and software vendors to capitalize on the current infatuation with the principles of CRM, there are those who have come to believe that relationship marketing is something you can buy off the shelf. It most definitely is not. CRM is not a technology. Effective CRM begins with the acknowledgment that it is a core value of the company. It is a commitment, an attitude and a focus that begins at the highest level of management and flows through the entire organization. CRM can and should be a significant ingredient in a company's overall marketing strategy. It is created by careful planning, thoughtful implementation and ongoing process improvement. Properly executed, it can literally make the difference between success and failure.

The tools made available to us in the Information Age have made it possible to achieve high levels of satisfaction among vast numbers of consumers. Nevertheless, it is still a highly personal process. As Jeff Multz, VP of Sales & Marketing for Firstwave software put it recently, "CRM is not a technology. At it's core it is a one-to-one interaction between two people."[16]

It is personal, individualized service given to each and every customer that makes CRM work. If we accept that premise, technology is seen for what it is, an implementation tool, not an answer unto itself. Ideally, it provides the ability to make effective use of customer demographics and create marketing tactics accordingly.

Finally, it pays to remember that the person most likely to spend money with you is someone who already has.

The Role of Customer Service

The story is told of a man we'll call Bob. The victim of an automobile accident Bob unexpectedly finds himself at the pearly gates. Saint Peter greets him warmly and suggests he take a look around. A few minutes later Bob goes back to Saint Peter and says, "Listen, things look great here, everybody seems happy but I don't see much excitement. Do I have any other options?"

"Of course" St. Peter replies, "You can always choose Hell. In fact you're in luck. Today is visiting day down there. Take a look and then let us know where you want to spend eternity."

Instantly, Bob is standing at the doorway to Hell. The temperature is a bit warm but there is music playing, people are dancing, wearing bright clothes, swimming in the pool and drinking margaritas. "Gosh," Bob thinks to himself. "I could get used to the weather and these people seem to be having a lot more fun than those in heaven." He goes back to St. Peter and announces his decision.

The next morning Bob wakes up sweating profusely lying on a bed of nails. The temperature is scorching, unbearably hot. People are wandering around in obvious pain carrying heavy loads and crying out for water. Confused and terrified at his apparent fate Bob searches out the devil. "What's this all about?" he asks. "I was here yesterday and there was music playing, people were having fun and the booze was flowing. What's the deal?"

"Simple' the devil replies, 'Yesterday you were a prospect. Today you're a customer!"

The role of customer service is to, hopefully, prevent creating a marketplace full of Bobs. Buyer's remorse is an insidious thing. It spreads through both current and potential clients with amazing speed. People tell people of their experiences, for better or worse, especially if they are worse. In a market-driven environment where several companies are fighting for share the ultimate winners are almost always those who find a way to satisfy customers before, during and after the sale.

We have suggested that excellent customer service is one of the key ingredients in a successful energy marketing strategy. The type of service we are referring to goes far beyond basic call center operations that served the purpose in a regulated environment. We are talking about world-class, state-of-the-art, prompt, personalized service that builds credibility and positive customer perception.

Successful energy marketing depends upon more than achieving a minimum level of customer satisfaction. It requires the ability to develop and maintain close relationships with customers, their preferences, buying habits, lifestyle choices and so on. It is essential to become *proactively* involved with customers and provide open, easy access when they want to communicate with the company.

It is estimated that over 90% of all customer contact in the utilities industry occurs via telephone. To put it in a marketing context, over 90% of all opportunities to affect customer perception, for better or worse, are going to occur during a telephone call to your company's customer care center. The proper operation of this vital link to customers must be an integral part of overall strategy.

Brian Jopling, head of The Merchants Group in the UK defines call centers as, "…a major vehicle for winning and retaining customers on a proactive and organized basis.". If this sounds very much like the definition of a company's marketing department the coincidence is intentional. Those who fully grasp the power of customer service to affect business success see themselves at the leading edge of a new paradigm that will eventually become an integrated part of the company's overall marketing effort.

World class customer service is not a software package. It is not a physical facility staffed with temporary employees and it is seldom accomplished through outsourcing. To be a true differentiator in an open, highly competitive environment, customers must be able to reach a live operator with a minimum of waiting time and few, if any, automated prompts to choose from. Impossible? not at all. In Britain, service standard requirements that 90+% of all calls be answered by a live operator within 30 seconds are commonplace.

Great customer service comes from a dedicated team of motivated individuals, working in a user-friendly environment, with the tools and systems necessary to insure a positive experience for the caller/customer.

In order to accomplish this goal you must be able to control the call process from beginning to end. If you cannot control the process, you cannot control the level of service provided. There are three main ingredients:

1. Intellectual knowledge and competence
2. Technology and systems to support the desired outcome
3. Appropriate process management

In general, the more robust the process the more effective. It does not really matter if you are starting from scratch or re-working an existing system. Your first job must be to find out what the prospective customer believes is the appropriate level of service.

There are basic questions most consumers have never been asked before. They may include, but are not limited to, the following:

1. "When the lights go out, how soon do you expect them to come back on?"
2. "When you call us, how quickly do you expect us to answer the phone?
3. "Are you comfortable working with an automated attendant or must you speak to a live operator?
4. "Are you willing to use the Internet to correspond with us? And, if so, on what issues?"

Note that we are not stating we can necessarily meet their expectations, only that we want to determine what the customer's definition of what "Good Service" really is. If we fail to conduct this research we are managing by anecdote, not information.

At Scottish Hydro-Electric, for example, we discovered that the service standard was actually higher than customer expectations. The company's management team had created a performance standard that required 98% of all calls to be answered by a live operator within 30 seconds. This criteria, while well intentioned, created pressure on front line employees to terminate calls and move on to the next when average wait-times exceeded the standard. Relaxing the standard to 95% increased first call completion rates and improved overall satisfaction measurements.

In the U.S. we are more likely to hear complaints about automated attendants, confusing Interactive Voice Response (IVR) systems and hold times. A recent survey indicated that of the 10 top "Pet Peeves" voiced by customers number one was being put in queue and told, "Your call is important to us." every 30 seconds[17]. In both the U.S. and Britain, the key to achieving high customer satisfaction scores, and thus high levels of retention, is the ability of a customer service agent to resolve an issue or answer a question quickly and accurately during the first call.

Rule of thumb: **The more personal the interaction the higher the level of perceived service satisfaction**

The challenge: **To find the balance of human interface vs. technology that is appropriate for the company's goals and resources**

When SCANA Energy decided to enter the Georgia market one of the first things they did was conduct extensive customer research. They used that research to establish service level standards.

Standards help manage customer expectations by establishing basic levels of service customers can expect to receive. These expectations are set both in how customers are treated, (human service level standards) and how customer's problems are solved, (business service level standards).

The process of creating written standards has two main objectives. The first is to set an expectation for your own employees. This in effect guides employee behavior and creates a template that managers can use to supervise their staff. A written set of standards says to the employees, "These are the standards set by senior management in response to what customers have told us they expect." The second objective is to send a clear message throughout the organization that everyone in the company from the CEO to the meter readers are working towards that same standard of service. Properly implemented this practice builds a culture that provides a level of service customers can expect to receive every time they contact the company.

It is likely that existing providers may have a more difficult time implementing such a concept. It is much harder to change a corporate culture with 20 or more years of doing something a certain way than to create a new system from scratch. The "new kids on the block" may have an advantage over the "old guard" from this standpoint because they are able to approach the entire issue of customer service from an integrated marketing perspective.

Business reality dictates that you may not be able to meet 100% of all customer expectations. In some cases it is just not economically feasible for a company to spend the money required to accomplish a given level of service. The point is, when setting standards; we must listen to "The Voice of the Customer". It is not always possible to do what they request but it is important to listen, evaluate internal capabilities and find the balance appropriate to the company's objectives and resources.

A process must be created to implement performance standards on a daily basis once all levels of management agree upon them. Legendary quality guru Dr. Edward Demming and others have repeatedly proven it is far easier to manage process than people. If processes are specific and support the goals of the company, employees will usually rise to the challenge. Dr. Joseph Juran, a student and disciple of Dr. Demming, studied process in a number of industries. He concluded that **only 15% of most errors are under the employee's control. 85% were caused by inappropriate procedures and inadequate systems.**

Contrary to popular belief in the call center industry, most employees truly want to do a good job. It is almost always some combination of unworkable procedures, inadequate systems, environmental factors or ineffective management that keeps them from doing it.

Fred Hanna spent nearly 20 years with SCANA Energy, the last five of those as Vice President in charge of customer service. During his tenure Fred spent at least 50% of his time meeting with employees, either one-to-one or in groups. By contrast, we recently completed a consulting project for a 200+ seat call center in which most employees had never met the call center manager let alone key executives above her level. Hardly a recipe for good morale and high levels of motivation.

Ideally, the on-site manager uses a majority of his or her time to relate the agreed upon standards to the employees and insure they have the tools necessary to implement them.

In the words of Fred Hanna, "When meeting with our staff it was to tell them: 'Here is what our service standards are. Here is what our customers are saying. Here is how we are doing. Now, what can I do to help you meet our service standards?'. When you ask that question in a non-threatening way you get all kinds of information. Some examples:

"If my chair was more comfortable I believe I could do a better job of being nice to customers."

"If our computer system followed the natural flow of the call it would be easier and faster than our current system which forces us to ask the customer questions out of sequence and often questions they have answered previously."

Your employees will tell you what they need to support the company's efforts. Mostly, they just want to be part of the process."

When we polled the employees of Scottish Hydro-Electric about what changes they would like to see in their call center, the number one response was a request for live plants. This came ahead of numerous other issues we had expected to address. It sounds unbelievable but in the often gray, overcast city of Perth, Scotland where the center is located, the idea of having live plants in the building had great appeal. (The plants were delivered within a week.)

Frank Domurath of Call Center Professionals, Inc. created the graphic shown below to illustrate the inter-connection of employees, systems and procedures.[18]

Figure 3

A challenge facing traditional organizations is that of making the transition from treating customer service as a functional area to a process driven department. There are eight strategic business processes common to most energy providers:

1. Billing
2. Meter reading
3. Order fulfillment
4. Credit & collections
5. Emergency recovery
6. Business management
7. Information fulfillment
8. Value added goods & services

Each of these requires someone to own that process, that part of the overall mix. These individuals know where the process begins, where it ends, what results are intended and how their area of influence contributes to the company's agreed-upon service standards.

It is the job of the strategic planning team to identify those areas that require a process to implement and support the standards. Ideally, line managers can then manage the business process to meet the agreed upon standards.

In general, employees do not think in terms of process. Usually they say, "Here is my piece of work." The power of process thinking is that it changes the culture of the organization to believe, "My job is not just this one component. I am a participant in this entire process and although I may be doing my part right, if my neighbor is having trouble, it's my job to help him get it right.".

Meter reading is a good example. If the individual meter reader says to him or herself, "I read my route, my job's over for the day." and then returns to the office he or she is practicing functional thinking. In the process-driven environment, we may have a person who did not complete their route and the company will have to estimate the un-read meters. If the established service standard is to deliver an accurate bill 100% of the time, an estimate is not good enough. So, in this example, the first reader would pitch in and help the second complete the readings.

In this way, front-line employees are in touch with what the company has promised to deliver and their part in that process. It is equally important that the employees are informed on a regular basis that service standards are in fact derived from what customers have indicated they expect.

The bottom line is that if employees come to work each day and do not understand the overall process and their important role in it, they are unlikely to perform at a high level of competence. In a recent survey by Ernest & Young, 73% of all employees said they wanted and needed more information on their company in order to do a better job.

Do not be tempted at this point to think all the above is a hypothetical scenario. SCANA Energy implemented this very system when preparing for deregulation and in 1999 won the prestigious J.D.Power Award for customer satisfaction.

Sometimes the most significant things are very basic. In our view, great customer service comes from two things - just two. But they must be done well and consistently. The first is to solve the customer's problem and the second is to treat them well while doing it. It's what Jan Carlson called "moments of truth" in service competition.[19] A process that insures a satisfactory outcome for every customer encounter has a synergetic effect on perception that grows exponentially over time.

When setting standards it is important to avoid what might be called process terrorism. This is the ego-driven phenomenon which can occur when people start viewing their piece or functional part as more important than the overall process.

Process terrorism is essentially a *people* problem which typically happens higher up in the organization where office politics are more intense. It is another reason why creating internal processes from customer input is so important. As a rule, customer expectations are not that extreme. Most have basic expectations and this is what you must deliver on. As the process evolves keep asking questions at every step along the way. "Will this help solve the customer's problem?" and "Will this enable our people to treat the customer fairly and with a good attitude?"

Well-designed process helps employees understand how their jobs fit in with the overall goal of meeting customer expectations. It encourages your staff to understand they are a vital link in delivering agreed upon service standards. To be credible, the process created must accurately reflect the company's core values.

We reflect here on the story of the tourist out for a morning walk in a European city who comes across a brick mason at work. "What are you doing?" asked the tourist. "Why, as you can see, I'm laying brick." was the reply. Later in the day another tourist passed the site and a different mason was hard at work. Again the question was asked, "What are you doing?" "Ah," the man answered with a smile. "I am building a cathedral."

The first mason was taking the functional view. "I am laying bricks." The second saw the beauty of the entire project. "I am building a cathedral." This is the process view.

Front line employees, like craft employees, can relate to that. Given the right tools and support they can say, "I'm not just reading meters" or "I'm not just listening to customer complaints all day." The attitude becomes instead, "I am helping build relationships between our company and our customers."

This philosophy was backed up with financial incentives at SCANA Energy. A bonus of $ 50.00 was paid to meter readers for each month with two or fewer reported errors per thousand. $ 100.00 was the reward for one or less errors. The expense is easy to justify. At the time SCANA was billing over 1.5 million customers. An error rate of even one percent adds up to a lot of customers. At an average cost of $ 50.00 per complaint, the small amount paid to front-line staff resulted in considerable savings to the company.

If you can grow a process-oriented belief system through the leadership of your supervisory team you will develop dedicated, highly effective front-line employees. And after all, nearly every customer transaction ultimately takes place on the front line.

Traditional call center operations too often rely primarily upon numbers to evaluate employee performance. If the goal is to build lasting customer relationships and use CRM as part of an overall marketing strategy this practice can be counter-productive. No less a luminary than Albert Einstein said, "Much of what we measure has no meaning. Much of what has meaning, we do not measure."[20].

The typical measurements of calls taken per hour or speed of completing the call may not in fact support the established service standard. In the process driven environment we measure *for desired results*, not just raw call volume numbers. It is essential to develop a mix of internal and external metrics that will support the ongoing process of managing quality as well as quantity.

Marketing professionals striving to achieve long term results may well encounter the classic dilemma of the service business, that being the perception of a customer care center as a cost center rather than a profit center. In most customer service budgets, billing and collections, emergency recovery, information fulfillment and so forth will usually be 60-70 cents of every dollar spent. To raise the level of accessibility and service means adding more personnel and usually more support systems. The key is to consistently provide senior management the correlation between increased budgets and bottom line profit improvement.

Companies that score significantly higher on customer satisfaction and loyalty typically have a higher return on market to book value than those in the same industry with lower quality scores. There is a direct, quantifiable connection between customer loyalty and long-term profits.

Frederick Riechheld's book uses the example of State Farm Insurance where a one percent increase in annual retention of policy holders added a billion dollars to its capital surplus. A billion dollars! Those kind of numbers get anyone's attention.

We encountered an all-too-familiar theme during a recent consulting project. "Our managers have no credibility at all," one employee told us. "They have signs everywhere talking about quality service and the customer being Number One but all my supervisor cares about is how many calls I take. The more calls, the better. Nobody really cares what happens on those calls, just that we take a lot of them!"

Here we come face to face with a hard truth. It is far easier to manage numbers than people. Computer printouts don't get sick, have fights with their significant others or arrive tired from too little sleep. They just are what they are, day-in and day-out. The skill set required to read, digest and create reports from raw numbers is far different from that required to coach, encourage and motivate a diverse group of human beings.

Harvard University's renowned management guru, Dr. Peter Drucker, is quoted as saying, "So much of what we call management consists of making it difficult for people to work."[21]. The beauty of a well thought-out process is that management becomes focused on managing that process to the level at which results meet the service standard.

Motivation can come in many forms. At SCANA Energy and several other progressive companies, financial rewards and recognition are given for meeting performance standards. As Fred Hanna likes to say, "You can't just talk corporate culture, you have to invest some money into it." However, it might be surprising to learn how little actual cash is required. Recognition can come in many forms; movie tickets, helium balloons, certificates of merit and many other inexpensive perks. All have proven highly effective. Key point: ***It is not the item or the money that is the motivator. It is the recognition.***

David Steele, Vice President, Marketing and Customer Services for Citizens Gas of Indianapolis, believes in managing by education and support rather by rules and enforcement. "The leaders job," Steele says, "is to create the environment for people to be successful in." [22]

Customer service operations that have both high morale and low employee turnover share most if not all of these ingredients:

1. The working environment is friendly, relaxed, open and vibrant
2. Work stations are bright, colorful and comfortable
3. Managers and employees alike engage in good-natured play (birthday parties, employee sponsored events, decorating for holidays, etc.)
4. Employees have considerable latitude and authority to solve customer problems
5. There is a feeling of common purpose among team members
6. Managers act as coaches and trainers rather than enforcers of rules and regulations

The product we are selling is essentially a service and a generic one at that. We must provide superior customer service the first time, every time if it is to be an integral part of overall marketing strategy. After contacting your company the only thing a customer has left is a memory. **A positive memorable customer experience is among the most powerful marketing tools in existence.**

Conversely, according to The Research Institute of America, 96% of unhappy customers never complain but 91% stop doing business with the company whom they believe treated them discourteously.[23]

The Question of Outsourcing

✹

If an energy company is to successfully compete over the long term, it must pay close attention to the fundamentals. With competition comes the requirement to examine every area of cost, calculate ROI and justify decisions as never before. Consequently, the idea of outsourcing the customer contact center inevitably is discussed and considered.

The fundamental issue is one of control. You must be able to manage the customer contact process with a high degree of consistency and predictability as to what level of service the customer will receive.

If you cannot control the process, you cannot manage the relationship.

Without process you cannot control the service level, you cannot control the transaction and you cannot control the outcome. Three factors are critical to the process:

1. You and your people must have intellectual knowledge of and confidence in the process
2. You must have technology and systems to support the process
3. You must have people who understand how to manage the process, the key measures of the process and the roles important to the process.

Outsourcing is a benefit only if it is invisible to the customer and the perceived level of service is at least as good as that provided by an in-house operation. The contractual agreement with an outsource provider must be absolutely clear as to what results are expected, what is measured and how the statistics generated by that measurement are utilized.

As stated previously, a chronic problem of call center operations is the tendency to measure the wrong things. The advent of computerized telephone systems brought the ability to measure a customer service representative's call volume, length of call, time available to accept calls and so on. Unfortunately, from a marketing and relationship-building perspective, these traditional measurements are often counterproductive.

Delegating customer relationship management to a third party requires that the processes created to achieve a specific level of service must be even more robust than what is required when doing it in-house.

For example, if it is determined that a particular process or policy is not working, it can be corrected almost immediately if the company is in total, daily control of the call center environment. On the other hand, if the function were outsourced, the vendor would be only obligated to perform what has been contractually agreed upon in advance.

To be fair, there are excellent contract call center operations that remain flexible to their customers' changing needs and are willing to adapt as necessary despite the language of the contract. On the other hand we have seen real horror stories of companies where long-term contracts have been signed **with no agreed upon performance standards at all!** This may have achieved some short-term cost savings but it is doubtful any company can retain their competitive advantage by placing their most valuable asset, their customer base, in the hands of a vendor over whom they have little control.

The best call center strategy, especially in the early days of open competition, may be a hybrid of both in-house and outsource segregated by call type, call volume, day-part or some combination of the three. For example, if a company wishes to promote 24/7 customer support as a competitive differentiator and it is known that very few calls are actually placed at night, the company might contract to have all calls between 6:00 PM and 6:00 AM handled by a third party.

Another possible use of an outsource vendor would be to answer customer inquires as the initial advertising campaign begins creating, (hopefully) hundreds or thousands of calls, well above what the number that will occur once the market settles down and the initial run of customers selecting an energy provider diminishes. It is not economically justifiable to hire and train a staff to handle the first few months of open competition knowing full well that call volumes will undoubtedly taper off to a more predictable level at some time in the future.

The good news is that reputable outsource vendors can be located anywhere in the country, or the world for that matter. Our experience indicates that in this area, as in so many things, you generally get what you pay for. While labor rates vary widely from state to state, the basic costs of doing business remain fairly constant. A high quality outsource company has all the same issues you would encounter handling 100% of calls in-house. If you do choose to outsource all or part of your customer relations' function, we suggest you consider the following guidelines.

1. Do not sign a long-term contract no matter how appealing the rate may be.
2. Specify what performance standards are expected in minute detail and in writing.
3. Have a written agreement outlining what results are desired and how they will be measured.
4. Plan to have a company employee at the vendor's site either full-time or at specified intervals to coach and train their operators on your policies and processes. The ideal outsource company employee should be a clone of your own internal staff.

There is much written in the trade press about specifications for service levels. Again, we are not speaking of raw numbers here but actual service as perceived by the customer. We believe it is nonsense to argue that it is not possible to specify a level of service perception. Of course you can!

Any product has tangible specifications. This bar of soap is so long and so wide. That box of cereal contains just so many ounces of product. This refrigerator contains a given number of cubic feet. The important thing about specifying a specific level of service is that we understand the parameters well enough to specify them. From a marketing perspective, the potential customer must understand and believe that he or she will receive a given level of service well enough to pay for it.

A caveat: the general public is usually unaware of the disconnect between inbound call center activity and physical, in the field service delivery. The consumer's perception of service quality is formed by the treatment received when they call to arrange new service or voice a complaint. Half-hour hold times and indifferent operators do not build customer loyalty. Remember also that when different companies are responsible for the sales function and infrastructure, consumers seldom understand the difference.

An often-heard comment in the early days of Georgia's natural gas deregulation was, "I called to sign up for company X's gas service and had to wait over 20 minutes for an operator. What if I had a gas leak? Would it take them over 20 minutes to answer the phone?" The problem was resolved by a simple change in menu options. Instead of the usual, "Thank you for calling brand X. Your call is important to us, please hold." the message became, "Thank you for calling. If you have a gas leak or other service problem, please press one now. To apply for new service or inquire about your bill, please press two." Pressing number one immediately bridged the call to the actual service provider.

When Shell Energy entered the Georgia market they outsourced the entire inbound call function. As a well recognized brand in motor fuels and lubricants Shell had the advantage of built-in credibility when selling home energy. Combined with Shell's corporate resources and significant natural gas reserves they were a powerful competitor.

Shells' decision to outsource their customer service function does contain an element of risk. If the outsource vendor does not provide a high level of service, is unable to handle peak call volumes in a time acceptable to customers or otherwise fails to support the sales effort appropriately, there is the potential for negatively impacting Shell's other product lines and services.

This proved to be the case during a peak period early in 2001 when average gas bills soared and inbound call volumes for all vendors increased dramatically. After numerous calls to Shell's toll-free number resulted in, "I'm sorry, due to heavy call volume we are unable to answer at this time." followed by a disconnection, many customers understandably took their business elsewhere. Will that same negative attitude extend to their buying habits when time comes to fuel the family car? That is the disturbing question.

Customer perception is a critical and delicate thing to manage. It takes years of hard work, creative advertising and promotion and consistently good service to create positive brand awareness. It takes only one bad experience to tear it down. Both anecdotal and statistical evidence suggests that a dissatisfied customer will delight in telling at least 10 others of his or her experience.

The question of outsourcing then is one of corporate culture and commitment. If aggressive, ongoing customer relationship management is to be part of the overall marketing effort, and we believe it should be, can the vital function of an inbound call center be handled externally? Is there a balance of in-house and outsourced functions that achieve the company's objectives while keeping costs at an appropriate and manageable level? And, in the final analysis, are you seeking short-term sales or long-term customer relationships?

We take the position that properly managed outsourcing can be a viable strategic choice. It is not a substitute for corporate commitment to the customer service process. It is not a way to eliminate the internal perception that customer service is a cost center and by moving it to an outside supplier costs will be reduced.

The professional marketer, in coordination with those responsible for customer satisfaction, will evaluate average customer lifetime value to the company and weigh that figure against the cost of providing world-class service. Only then can a thoughtful, reasoned decision be made about which course of action is warranted.

Final Thoughts and Observations

✸

It is a paradox. Attributes that have contributed to the success of energy providers have the potential to make them strong competitors in an era of open competition. Energy companies as a group are typically more conservative in their executive decision making and have historically been more financially stable than many other industries. Senior managers are more likely to understand the viability of investing in strategies whose benefits may take months or years to be fully recognized.

Conversely, deregulation presents an entirely new set of parameters in which to operate. It requires a significant shift in the way customers are attracted, service offerings are packaged and customer service is administered. Cultural behavior patterns that have evolved over decades are seldom appropriate to the new reality. Energy retailers must adopt an entirely new way of doing business to be successful. They must create an organizational paradigm appropriate to the future which is dramatically different from that which worked so well in the past.

It is a common theme in management literature that fundamental cultural change is the most difficult challenge faced by any organization. Human beings by nature, regardless of age, intelligence or position, cling to what is familiar. For organizations to change, the people must change. Employees at all levels bound by historical "truths" neither valid nor appropriate, become uncomfortable as emerging competitive reality demands new, unfamiliar professional competence and behavior.

The energy industry is entering a period of transition unique in its history. Many in the business are struggling with uncertainty, fear, distrust and an inclination to cling to what is known. The last of these, clinging to past methods and behaviors, is the most difficult to address and resolve.

General Electric's Jack Welch states, "The art of managing and leading comes down to a simple thing. Determining and facing REALITY, about people, situations, products and then acting decisively and quickly on that reality."[24]

Senior managers of energy companies who embrace the reality of operating in a deregulated environment and are willing to approach the business from a totally new perspective are the ones most likely to succeed.

Likewise, the future of marketing is going to be very different from that experienced in the last century or even the last decade. Companies can no longer create a marketing budget, entrust it to some person or department and hope for desired results in an increasingly competitive world

The successful marketing professional will be aware of the following trends and include them in his or her strategic thinking:

- Relationship building over time with an emphasis on CLV
- Increased accountability of expenditures vs. sales results
- Emphasis on convenience /value/price relationships
- Individualized attention as a differentiation strategy
- Ever more specialized demographic targeting
- One-to-one and one-on-one service
- Increasingly international
- Increasingly "cashless"
- Mass customization

A combination of branding, aggressive sales promotion, bundling of services, strategic partnerships and relationship marketing (or CRM) appear to be the most effective choices for energy suppliers. These ingredients create a powerful synergy. The holistic; quality/sales/customer service approach is well suited to the industry.

Customer lifetime value is relatively easy to track given the ongoing, everyday nature of the supplier/customer relationship and the necessity of maintaining a comprehensive, up-to-date data base for metering, billing and service. Energy companies can raise overall customer awareness and create additional profit opportunities by forming strategic alliances with non-competing enterprises.

We are entering a new era in service competition. It is an exciting, challenging time. We are moving uncertainly, ever so cautiously, towards total deregulation, state-by-state, municipality-by-municipality. Ultimate success in this environment will require a combination of long-term strategic planning, marketing expertise and an unwavering commitment to exceptional customer service.

We sincerely hope this work will contribute to your ultimate success.

1. Time, Vol. 157, No. 4, January 29, 2001, pages 36 - 44
2. Author's Note: The Georgia Public Service Commission considers market share information confidential which precludes us from including up-to-date statistics.
3. Samuelson, Robert J. "*California's Energy Circus*", Newsweek, July 18, 2001, p. 37
4. USA Today, June 18, 2001, page 2A
5. Mayle, Peter, *Up the Agency*, 1990 Pan Books, Ltd.
6. Rubin, Harriet, *Soloing*, HarperCollins, 1999
7. Darby, Warren, personal interviews May 12, 2001 & June 2, 2001
8. Goldman, Mark - Personal interview conducted June 4, 2001
9. *The Wall Street Journal*, May 17, 1999
10. "*Your Company and Customer Care*", Smith Bundy and Partners
11. Gronroos, Christian, *Managing the Moments of Truth in Service Competition*, Free Press /Lexington Books 1990
12. Martin, P. "*The Death of Geography*", Financial Times, 13 June, 1996
13. Reichheld, Frederick, F. *The Loyalty Effect*, Bain & Company, Inc., 1996
14. Reichheld, Frederick, F. *The Loyalty Effect*, Bain & Company, Inc., 1996
15. Anton, Jon, et al, *Customer Relationship Management*, Prentice Hall, 1996
16. Multz, Jeffery, address to the Atlanta Marketing Forum, February 19, 2001
17. Bond, Chris & Camack, Mark "*Your Call Is Important to Us...Please Hold*", Ergonomics in Design, October, 1999
18. Copyright 2000 by Frank Domurath, president, Call Center Professionals, Inc. used with permission
19. Jan Carlson is the CEO of Scandinavian Airlines
20. Drummond, James, "*Monitoring & Quality Programs for Call Centers*", IQPC, February 11, 1999
21. Drucker, P. "*Leading from a distance*", Call Center Focus, No. 1, May/June, 1997
22. Steele, David E. address to the Midwest Energy Association, April 5, 2001
23. Knox, Nolle, *USA Today*, June 28, 2001, page 7B
24. Slater, Robert, *Get Better or Get Beaten*, Irwin Professional Publishing, 1994

LIST OF RESOURCES

Mr. Jim Drummond
Managing Director
Drummond Consulting, Ltd.
jimd@drummondconsulting.net
770-248-0210

Mr. Fred Hanna
Senior Consultant, Customer Service
Drummond Consulting, Ltd.
fredh@drummondconsulting.net
803-446-4912

Ms. Lisa Dawn Holmer
Vice President, Market Development
Drummond Consulting, Ltd.
lisah@drummondconsulting.net
425-344-1360

Mr. Frank Domurath
President
Call Center Professionals, Inc.
fdomurath@aol.com
248-623-4991

SUGGESTED READING

Anton, Jon, Monger, J. et al, *Customer Relationship Management*, Prentice-Hall, Inc.

Christopher, M., Payne, A. & Ballantyne, D., *Relationship Marketing*, Butterworth/Heinemann

Davidson, Hugh, *"Offensive Marketing"* & *"Even More Offensive Marketing"*, Penguin Business Press

Davidson, W., and Uttal, B., *Total Customer Service: The Ultimate Weapon*, Harper & Row

Morton, C., *Becoming World Class*, Macmillian Press

Peppers, D. and Rogers, M., *Enterprise One to One: Tools for Competing in the Interactive Age*, Currency/Doubleday

Reichheld, Frederick, *The Loyalty Effect*, Harvard Business School Press

ABOUT THE AUTHORS

James H. (Jim) Drummond is Managing Director of Drummond Consulting, Ltd. an international management advisory firm based in Atlanta, Georgia.

Prior to the establishment of his consulting practice Jim spent 20 years directing sales and marketing strategy for several international companies including Canon USA and Sony Corporation. As a consultant he has created highly successful campaigns for both consumer and business to business clients in the United States and Great Britain. He has advised several U.S. utilities on the challenges of open competition and the importance of CRM in overall marketing strategy.

Jim spent 1997 in Scotland working with Scottish Hydro-Electric, (now Scottish & Southern Energy) as they prepared for deregulation. He was an invited speaker at the 1999 joint conference of the Edison Electric Institute and American Gas Association.

David Sigsworth, Commercial Director of Scottish Hydro-Electric called Jim's work, "…a unique combination of marketing expertise, management ability, insight and creativity."

A highly regarded public speaker Jim serves on the invited faculty of Purdue University's Center for Customer Driven Quality and makes personal appearances to professional associations and trade groups on the subjects of marketing and customer relationship management.

Jim did his undergraduate work in communications at the University of Florida and received his MBA from the University of Edinburgh with an emphasis in marketing and strategic planning.

jimd@drummondconsulting.net

Fred N. Hanna is Senior Consultant, Customer Service for Drummond Consulting, Ltd.

His career spans over two decades in the utilities industry, most recently as Vice President of Customer Service for SCANA Energy. Fred has extensive experience in all facets of customer service, strategic planning, process improvement, systems implementation, project and change management. He has been voted the industry's "Outstanding Manager" by Gas Industries Magazine. Fred designed the process improvement system which led to SCANA's selection as recipient of the J.D. Power Award for Customer Satisfaction in 1999.

Fred Hanna graduated from Clemson University with a Bachelor of Engineering degree. He has served as Vice Chairman of the AGA/EEI Customer Service Committee, as a member of the Southeastern Electric Exchange Customer Service and Accounting Committee and on two advisory boards for Clemson University.

fredh@drummondconsulting.net

www.ingramcontent.com/pod-product-compliance
Lightning Source LLC
Chambersburg PA
CBHW021016180526
45163CB00005B/1979